Police Dogs

WORKING DOGS

By Mary Ann Hoffman

Gareth Stevens
Publishing

Please visit our Web site, www.garethstevens.com. For a free color catalog of all our high-quality books, call toll free 1-800-542-2595 or fax 1-877-542-2596.

Library of Congress Cataloging-in-Publication Data

Hoffman, Mary Ann, 1947-
Police dogs / Mary Ann Hoffman.
    p. cm. — (Working dogs)
Includes index.
ISBN 978-1-4339-4660-8 (pbk.)
ISBN 978-1-4339-4661-5 (6-pack)
ISBN 978-1-4339-4659-2 (library binding)
1. Police dogs—Juvenile literature. 2. Police dogs—Training—Juvenile literature. I. Title.
HV8025.H64 2011
363.28—dc22

2010035244

First Edition

Published in 2011 by
Gareth Stevens Publishing
111 East 14th Street, Suite 349
New York, NY 10003

Designer: Michael J. Flynn
Editor: Kristen Rajczak

Photo credits: Cover, p. 1 Heather Weston/Botanica/Getty Images; pp. 5, 6, 10, 13, 14, 17, 18, 20 Shutterstock.com; p. 9 iStockphoto.com.

Printed in the United States of America

CPSIA compliance information: Batch #CW11GS: For further information contact Gareth Stevens, New York, New York at 1-800-542-2595.

Contents

Words in the glossary appear in **bold** type the first time they are used in the text.

Special Skills

Police dogs have special skills. They're smart, strong, **loyal**, and have excellent senses of smell and hearing. Police dogs have become very important and necessary in police work. They track down **suspects**. They keep people under control. They find things that are hidden. They search for people and lost objects. Let's read about police dogs and how they're trained.

4

Dog Tales

Some studies show that a dog's sense of smell can be 1,000 times greater than a person's! Dogs can also recognize one certain scent among many others.

This police dog is ready for work!

Dog Tales

The **relationship** between handler and police dog is very close. Handlers and their dogs often live together.

This police dog will listen to its handler's commands.

A Handler

Training police dogs takes skill and a calm manner. A handler is the person who trains the police dog. The handler is also responsible for taking care of the dog. The handler is in charge of the dog both on and off duty. Police dog handlers use voice commands. They also use sounds and hand signs to let the dog know what they want it to do.

Working Together

Each handler develops a close, positive working relationship with their dog. The handler continues training their dog throughout the relationship. Training a police dog means building trust between handler and dog. A police dog is trained to follow only commands given by its handler. The handler must be **physically fit** since the handler and dog work as a team.

Dog Tales

A police dog and its handler form a K-9 unit. "K-9" comes from the word "canine," which is another word for dog.

This police officer is telling his dog what to do by giving it a hand sign.

Dog Tales

The handler is the only person who does basic training with the dog.

Police dogs have to learn how and when to be forceful. ▷

Basic Training

All police dogs go through basic training. Training in special skills comes later. Basic training is usually done when the dog is a puppy, so the dog and handler become comfortable with each other. The dog learns that its handler is in charge. Basic training includes **obedience** and simple **behavior** exercises. Police dogs are trained to follow clear commands that control barking, biting, chewing, jumping, chasing, and running away.

Dog Tales

Breeds used as police dogs are very curious and like to learn new things. They have sharp senses of smell and sight.

The German shepherd is one of the most common police dogs.

German Shepherds

Several dog breeds make very good police dogs. Let's read about some of the most common kinds.

German shepherds are medium-sized, active dogs. They're smart, strong, quick, and have a sharp sense of smell. They like to learn new things and can be easily trained to perform many different tasks. German shepherds are loyal, protective, and obedient to their handlers.

Rottweilers

Rottweilers are **muscular**, powerful dogs often used as police dogs. Rottweilers like to be active. They like to have a job to do. They're smart and have a lot of **stamina**. Rottweilers are dependable, calm, and watchful. They're very protective of their territory and their owner. Basic obedience training and mixing with people and other dogs are important for these dogs. Rottweilers are easily trained to swiftly follow commands. They're fearless in their loyalty.

Dog Tales

There are rottweiler clubs all over the United States.

A rottweiler is easy to recognize. It's black with tan markings on its face, cheeks, chest, legs, and eyes.

17

Dog Tales

The Belgian Malinois looks a lot like a German shepherd, but it's a little smaller and faster.

The Belgian Malinois loves having a job to do.

Belgian Malinois

The Belgian Malinois is another popular police dog. This medium-sized dog is good at protection as well as locating things. It's strong, hardworking, active, and tireless. It likes to be **challenged**. The Belgian Malinois is smart. It enjoys learning new things. It can be easily trained to follow commands. It's thoughtful and watchful. It can be especially loyal to one person. The Belgian Malinois makes an excellent police dog.

Doberman Pinschers

Doberman pinschers, often just called Dobermans, are excellent as police dogs. They're very muscular. They enjoy being active and solving problems. Dobermans are quick to act. They're loyal, brave, and daring. They're easily trained and obedient. Because of these features, as well as their stamina and speed, Dobermans make outstanding police dogs when properly trained. They respect their handler's commands.

Police Dogs

Task	Activity
control and force	chase after and hold suspects
detection	find hidden objects such as drugs, explosives, or other materials
tracking	follow a trail to locate missing people or things

Glossary

behavior: how someone or something acts

breed: a group of animals that share features different from other groups of that kind

challenge: to test how well one does something

loyal: faithful

muscular: having powerful, strong muscles

obedience: the act of obeying

obstacle: something that blocks a path

physically fit: good control of moving the body

protect: keep someone or something safe from harm

relationship: connection between people, animals, or things

stamina: able to keep doing something without tiring

suspect: a person who may have broken the law

Books:

Bozzo, Linda. *Police Dog Heroes.* Berkeley Heights, NJ: Enslow Publishers, 2010.

Murray, Julie. *Crime-Fighting Animals.* Edina, MN: ABDO Publishers, 2009.

Stewart, Gail B. *K-9 Police Units.* Detroit, MI: Lucent Books, 2010.

Web Sites:

Canine Unit

www.troopers.state.ny.us/specialized_services/Canine_Unit

Learn about canine training and view pictures of police dogs.

Police K-9s Trained for the Street

www.tarheelcanine.com/police.cfm

Read about K-9 training and watch a video of handlers and dogs in action.

Index